Our Neighborhood Beyond the Solar System

A Beginners Guide

Caelix Publishing
Copyright © 2020

In our last edition; Our Neighborhood The Solar System, we took a look at the planets and moons that make up our Solar System. However, there is so much more out there! In this edition of "Our Neighborhood", we hope to pull back the curtain on some of the wonders that exist outside of our humble solar system for curious, young astronomers. This is merely a sneak-peek as to what is out there, and barely even scratches the surface of what makes up outer space!

COMETS

Comets are dirty snowballs of frozen gases and rocks that orbit our Sun. They are usually the size of a small town. When a comet's orbit brings it close to the sun, it heats up and lets off clouds of dust and gas that creates an extended atmosphere (called a Coma), growing to a size larger than most planets. In fact, the Comet known as Holmes has released so much gas and dust that its coma was larger than the size of the Sun. Wow!

Comets have very erratic orbits when compared to the planets in our solar system. Some comets have orbits that can last hundreds or even thousands of years. One of the most famous comets is Halley's Comet. It travels around the sun every 75 to 76 years. The last time Comet Halley visited the inner solar system was in 1986, so the next time we will be able to see it in our skies is in the middle of 2061.

Halley's Comet photographed in March 1986
Photo Courtesy of NASA

"Taking a Comet Temperature"
Comet 67P/Churyumov-Gerasimenko
Photo Courtesy of NASA

Another famous comet was Shoemaker-Levy 9. This comet was on a collision course with Jupiter the 1990's. In 1992, using telescopes, we were able to observe the comet breaking up, and finally in 1994 crashing into the planet Jupiter.

Comet Shoemaker-Levy 9
Approaching Jupiter in 1994
Photo Courtesy of NASA

One other famous comet is Oumuamua. Oumuamua passed through our Solar System in 2017, and was the first known interstellar object to pass through our Solar System. Despite passing fairly closely to the Sun, astronomers found it strange that this comet had no Coma.

Oumuamua Artist Concept
Image Courtesy of NASA

Kuiper Belt and the Oort Cloud

Image Courtesy of NASA

The Kuiper Belt is a relatively flat ring of ice and rock beyond the orbit of Neptune. It has many "ice" rocks that are made up of frozen gases like methane, ammonia, and water. It is home to the three currently known Dwarf Planets: Pluto, Makemake, and Humea. It is similar in makeup to the Asteroid Belt, but far, far larger. The Kuiper Belt extends out to approximately 50 AU's. One AU is the distance of the Sun to the Earth, about 93 million miles. It's pretty far out there!

The dwarf planet Pluto was originally considered the 9th planet in our Solar System, but was reclassified in 2006 as a Dwarf Planet after the discovery of other planetary bodies in the belt that were around the same size as Pluto. The first spacecraft to explore the Kuiper Belt was called New Horizons. The New Horizons probe visited Pluto, and Arrokoth; an oddly shaped object, about the size of a dwarf planet, in the Kuiper belt.

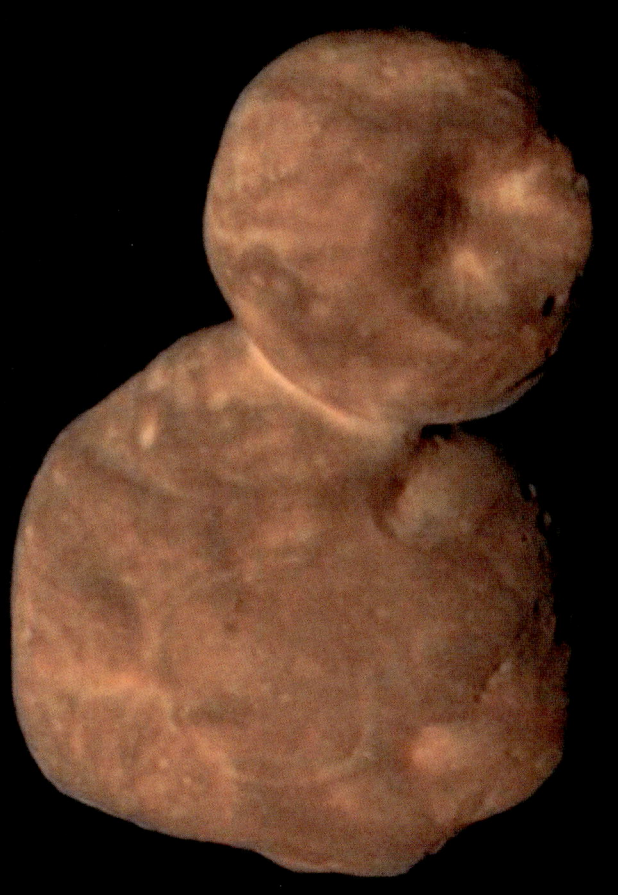

(Left) Arrokoth, the farthest object in our system to be photographed
(Right) Pluto
Both Photos Courtesy of NASA

Further out in the Solar System is the Oort Cloud. The Oort cloud is also a region of ice and rock that orbits our sun. However, unlike the Kuiper Belt, the Oort Cloud surrounds our entire solar system like a giant ball.

Voyager 1 and 2 Spacecraft

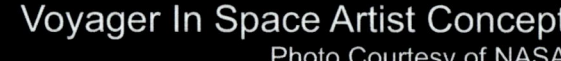

Voyager In Space Artist Concept
Photo Courtesy of NASA

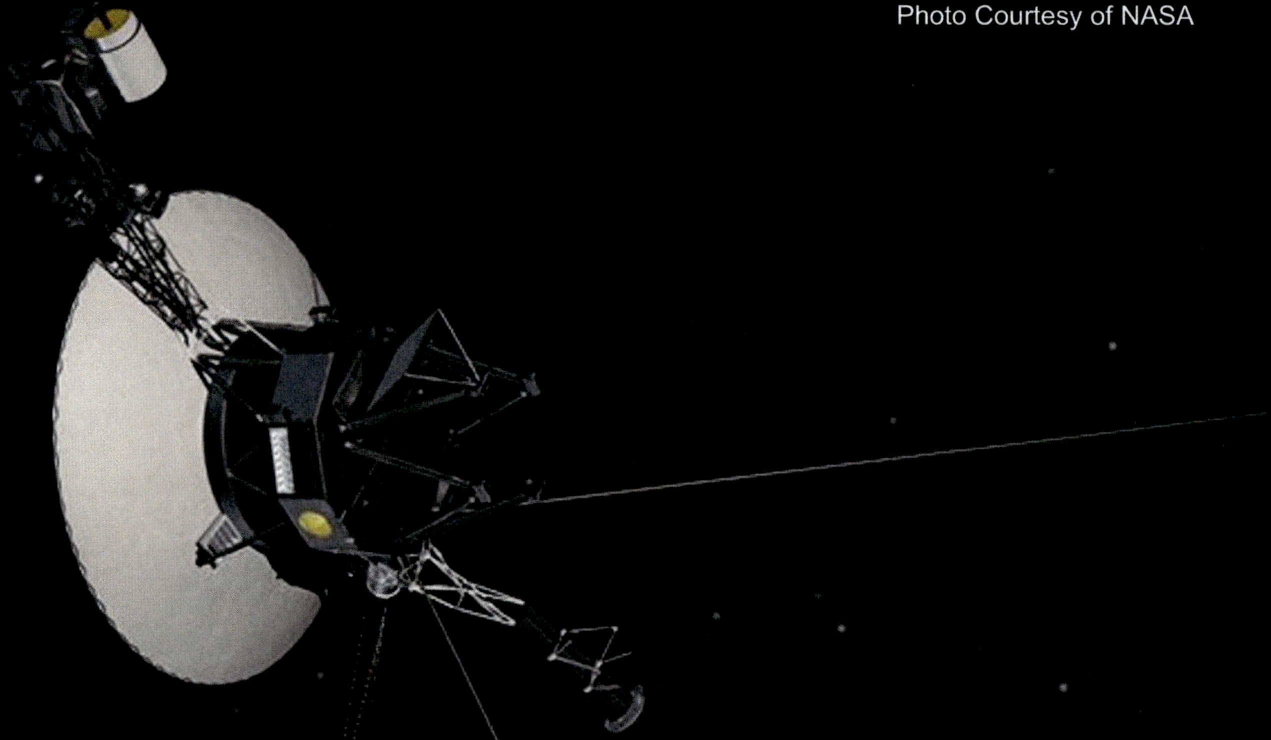

As we move out beyond the Kuiper Belt, we run into the most famous man made objects out in space, the Voyager Spacecrafts! Voyager 1 and Voyager 2 are the most distant spacecrafts launched from Earth, and they are both now in interstellar space. Using what is called the NASA Deep Space Network, you can track their exact location and velocity at this very moment at https://voyager.jpl.nasa.gov/mission/status/

Voyager 1 is a space probe launched on September 5th, 1977. The Voyager program was designed to explore the outer Solar System. Voyager 1's objectives included flyby's of Jupiter, Saturn, and Saturn's moon Titan, the only known moon to have an atmosphere of its own! On August 25th, 2012, Voyager 1 became the first spacecraft to cross the heliopause and enter interstellar space!

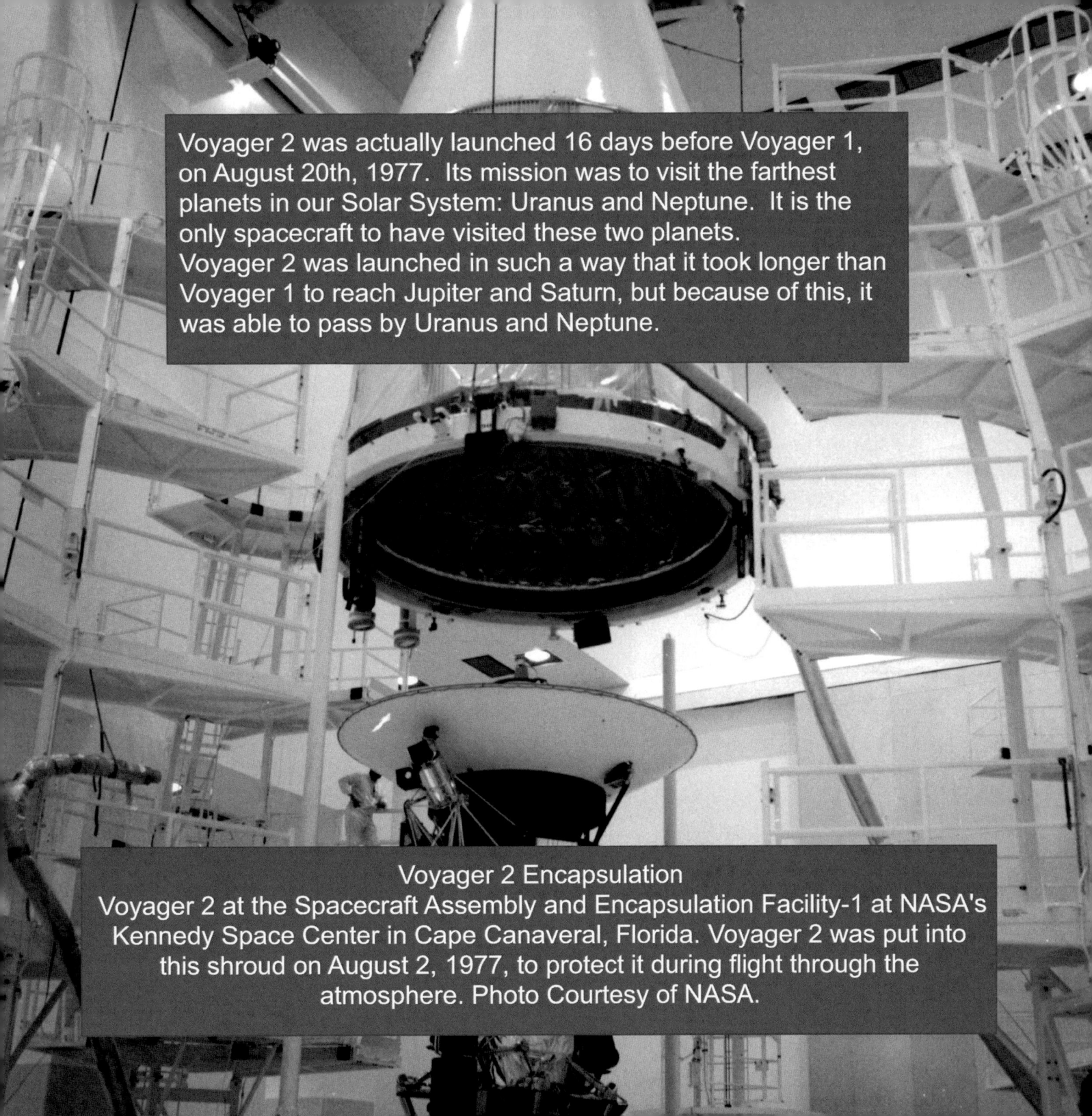

Voyager 2 was actually launched 16 days before Voyager 1, on August 20th, 1977. Its mission was to visit the farthest planets in our Solar System: Uranus and Neptune. It is the only spacecraft to have visited these two planets.
Voyager 2 was launched in such a way that it took longer than Voyager 1 to reach Jupiter and Saturn, but because of this, it was able to pass by Uranus and Neptune.

Voyager 2 Encapsulation
Voyager 2 at the Spacecraft Assembly and Encapsulation Facility-1 at NASA's Kennedy Space Center in Cape Canaveral, Florida. Voyager 2 was put into this shroud on August 2, 1977, to protect it during flight through the atmosphere. Photo Courtesy of NASA.

The historic moment when Voyager 2 was launched.

Photo Courtesy of NASA

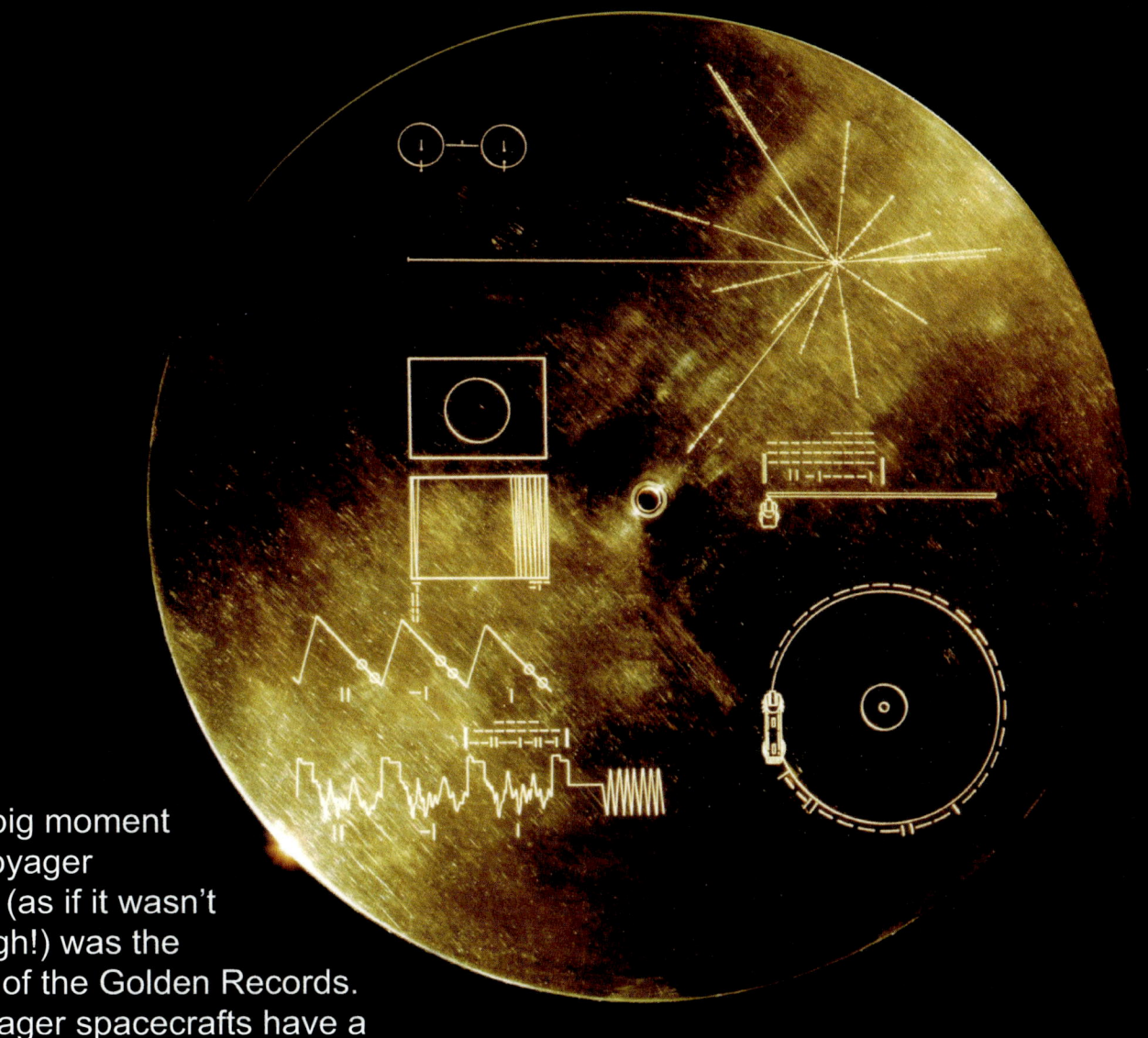

Another big moment for the Voyager launches (as if it wasn't big enough!) was the inclusion of the Golden Records. Both Voyager spacecrafts have a golden record that contains 115 images, natural sounds (thunder, animals, water, etc.), music from different cultures, and greetings in 55 different languages in the event that intelligent, extraterrestrial life find either of the spacecraft. Think of it as a mix between a time capsule, and showcase of humankind.

STARS

Stars are large bright spheres of gas and plasma that are held together by their own gravity. They are at the heart of all solar systems in the universe. Stars come in all shapes and sizes. There are also many colors of stars, such as Blue, Orange, Red, yellow, white. They range in size from small dwarf stars to incredibly huge hypergiants.

In order of size there are:
White Dwarf Stars. These stars are about the size of the Earth. The mass of these stars can equal that of our own Sun despite being so small.

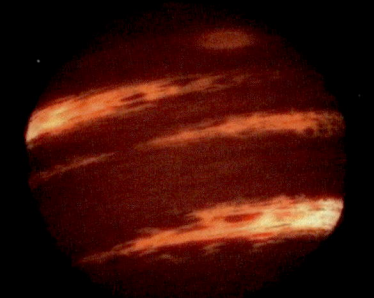

Brown Dwarf Stars: These are strange stars. They aren't big enough to be a star but are too big to be a planet. They simply don't have the mass to produce the fusion required to become a star. Scientists refer to Brown Dwarf stars as "failed stars".

Red Dwarf: Red dwarfs are among the most common stars in the universe. The closest star to our Sun , Proxima Centauri, is a red dwarf.

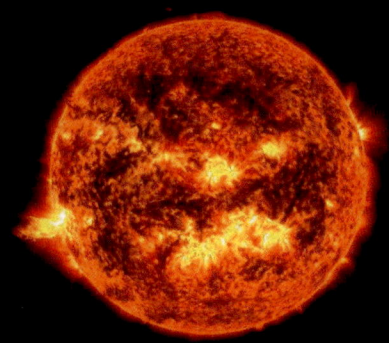

Yellow Dwarf: Our Sun is a yellow dwarf star. Yellow dwarfs are called "main sequence" stars because they are in the stable time of their life cycle.

They only get bigger from there! The next biggest stars are Blue Giant. Blue giants are considerably larger than Yellow Dwarfs and are very, very hot. Much hotter than our Sun. They are quite rare among the stars in the sky.

Yellow giants are stars that are larger than blue giants but are much cooler. They become inflated as they leave their main sequence and because they inflate, the temperature cools.

Red giants are huge bright stars that have low mass. Red giants are dying stars, getting close to the end of their life cycle. They may have once started as smaller dwarf stars, and they swell into red giants as they burn most of the hydrogen at their core.

Supergiants and Hypergiants are the largest and brightest stars out there. Their mass can range from 8 to 12 times the mass of our sun, and have a brightness of up to a million times more than our sun. They become blue supergiants through the pressure of radiation, convection, and large amounts of burning hydrogen. Red supergiants are a size in between red hypergiants and blue hypergiants. These stars become red supergiants when they use most of the hydrogen at their core and are entering the final stage of their life cycle.

This background image is of the Witch Head Nebula which contains the Blue Supergiant Rigel, which is one of the brightest stars in our night sky.

Photo Courtesy of NASA

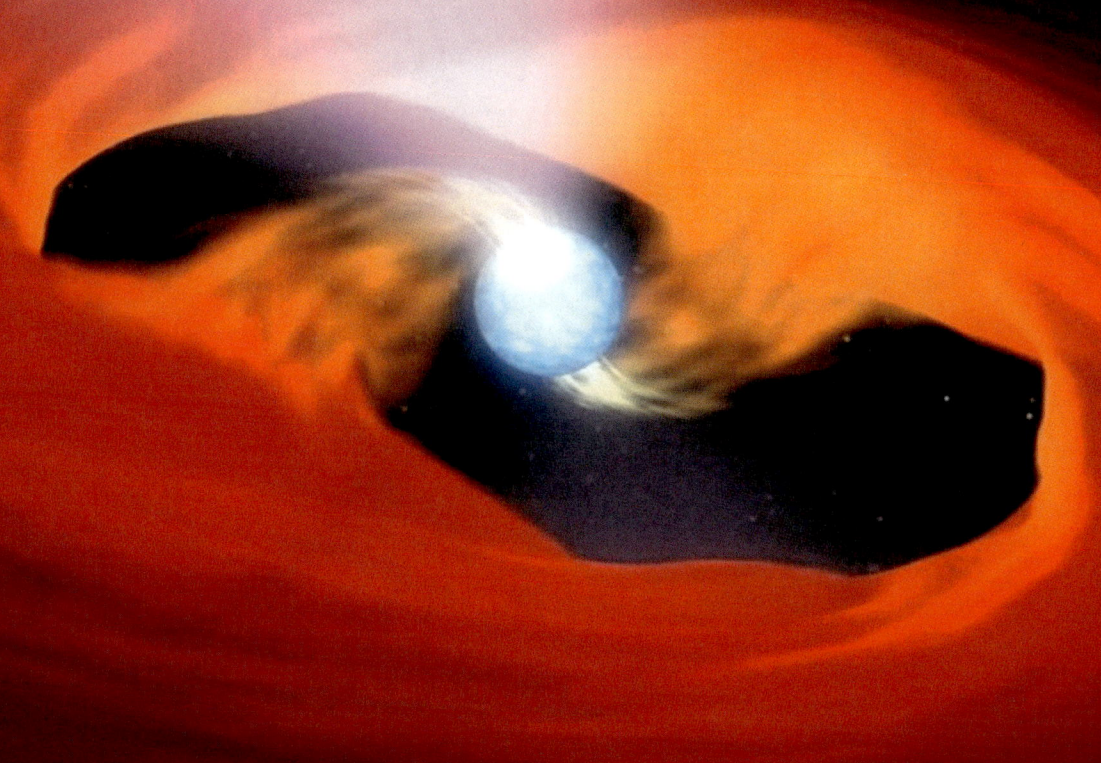

Neutron stars are special. They are the remnants of the core of a large star after they have exploded in a supernova, and collapsed in on themselves and the end of their life spans. Neutron stars can be very small: about 18 to 40 miles across. But they can also be very large Depending on the size of the star that collapsed.

"Beacons of X-ray Light Animation"
Image Courtesy of NASA

Alpha Centauri is the closest star system to ours, at around 4.37 light years away. A light year is the distance light travels in one year on Earth, about 6 trillion miles. The Alpha Centauri system has 3 stars in it: Alpha Centauri A, B, and Proxima Centauri. Proxima is the closest star to our solar system. In 2012, scientists discovered a planet orbiting Alpha Centauri B.

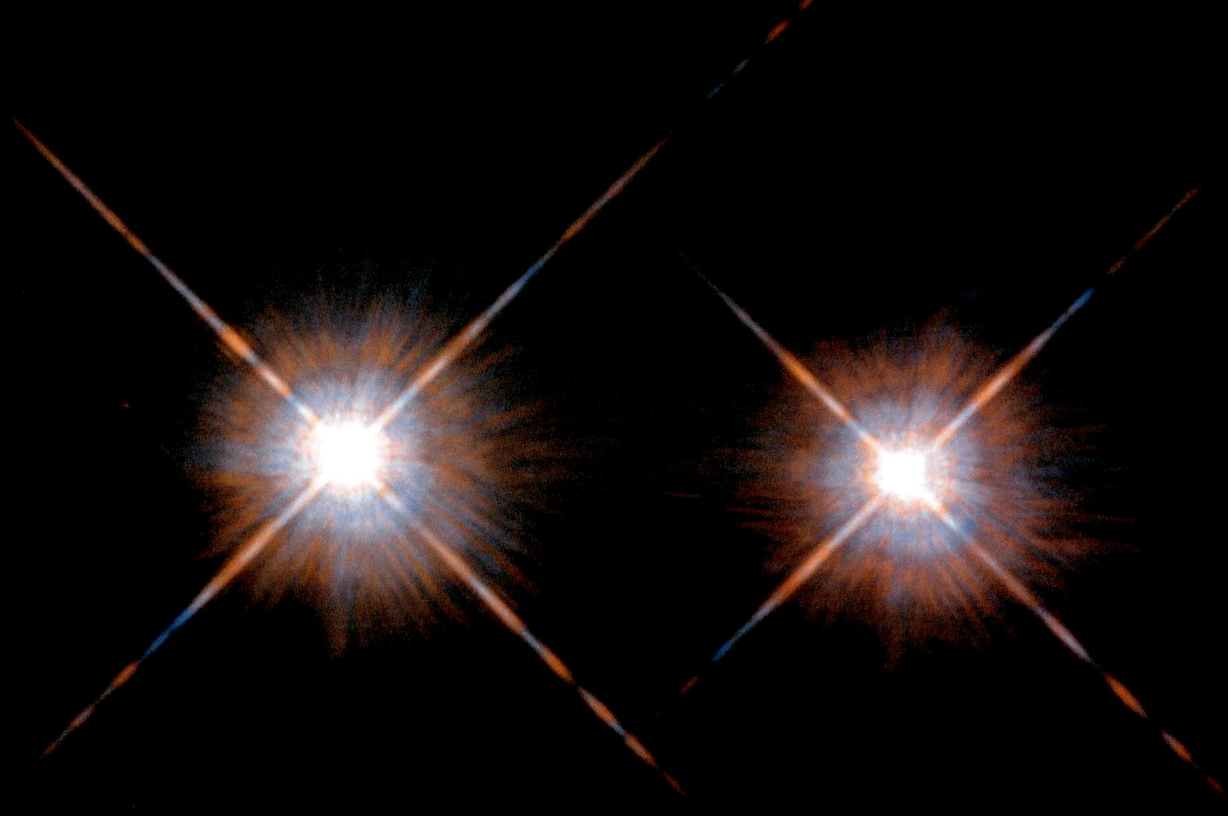

Alpha Centauri A and Alpha Centauri B, With Proxima Centauri barely visible on the left.
Photo Courtesy of NASA

NEBULAS

"Planetary Nebula NGC 7293 also known as the Helix Nebula"
Photo Courtesy of NASA

A nebula is a huge cloud of dust and gas that acts as a nursery for new stars. They are made up of dust, elements such as hydrogen and other ionized gases that eventually compress into stars. The closest nebula to us is the Helix Nebula, about 700 light years away.

NGC 1999: The reflection of a nebula in the Orion constellation.
This nebula does not actually produce any light of its own, and instead, reflects light from a nearby star, giving it its foggy appearance.

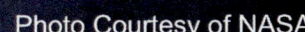

The Pillars of Creation
The Pillars of Creation are pillars of dust and gas at the heart of the Eagle Nebula, about 6,500 - 7,000 light years away from Earth.

Photo Courtesy of NASA

Carina Nebula
The Carina Nebula is one of the largest known star birthing regions in the universe. Seen here is a small portion of the Carina Nebula showing a three light year tall pillar of hydrogen and dust.

Photo Courtesy of NASA

GALAXIES

Galaxies are massive clusters of star systems, stellar remnants, interstellar gas, and dark matter that are held together by gravity, and come in all shapes and sizes. It is now believed that at the center of every galaxy is a supermassive black hole. Our galaxy, the Milky Way, is a spiral galaxy. On September 24th, 2003, the Hubble Space Telescope imaged what is now famously known as the "Hubble Deep Field". This picture showcased thousands of galaxies peering back to the beginnings of the universe.

Image from Hubble's Deep Field Telescope
Photo Courtesy of NASA

Andromeda
Photo Courtesy of NASA

The closest galaxy to ours, Andromeda, is a barred spiral galaxy, and it can be seen in the sky by the naked eye. It is 2.56 million light years away.

"The Triangulum"

The Triangulum is a galaxy nearly 3 million light years from Earth.

Photo Courtesy of NASA

NGC 1569 or the Starburst Galaxy
The Starburst Galaxy got its name because it creates stars faster than any other galaxy in our neighborhood, and is home to the three largest star clusters in the local universe.

Photo Courtesy of NASA

PULSARS

Pulsars are highly magnetized, rotating neutron stars. They emit beams of radiation out of both side of their cores, and because they are spinning, from Earth, they look like twinkling stars. Pulsars are left over stellar material from a star that collapsed in on itself, but was not large enough to form a black hole.

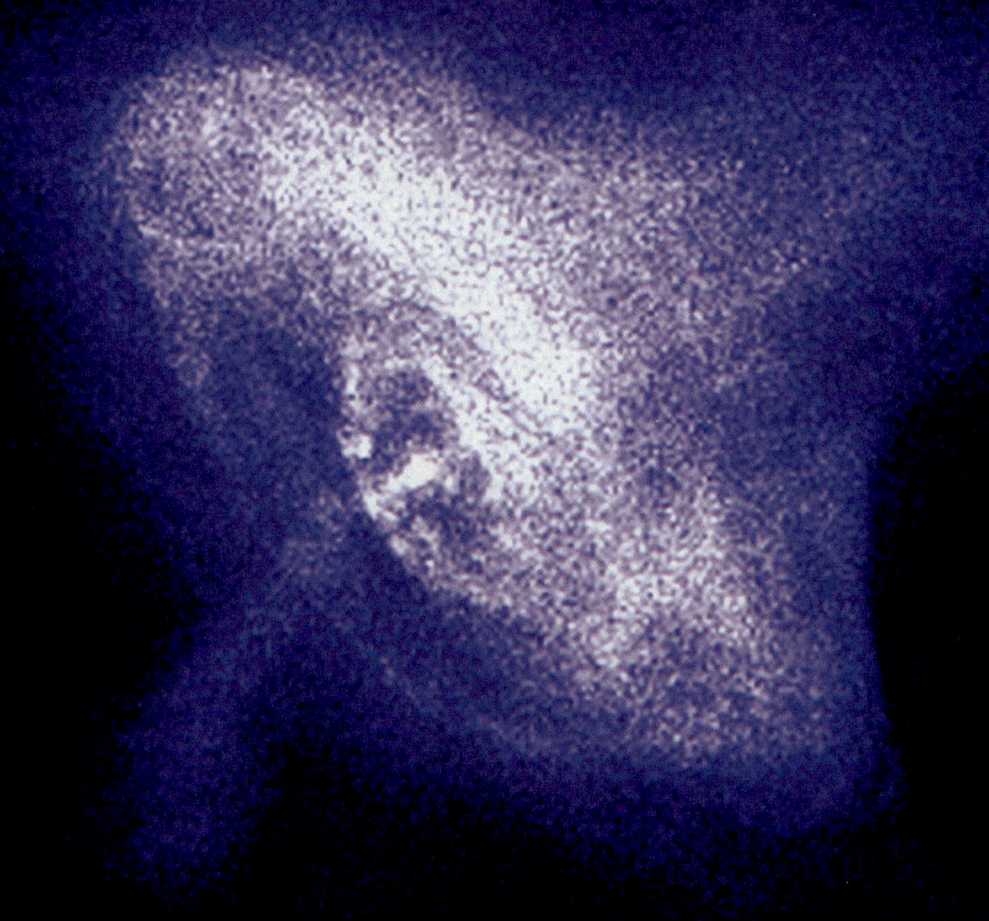

Photo Courtesy of NASA

SXP 1062 (The bright white spot on the right side of the image): This pulsar, located in the remains of a supernova, has been interesting to astronomers because it rotates unusually slow; about once every 18 minutes. Most pulsars rotate multiple times in a single second!

Photo Courtesy of NASA

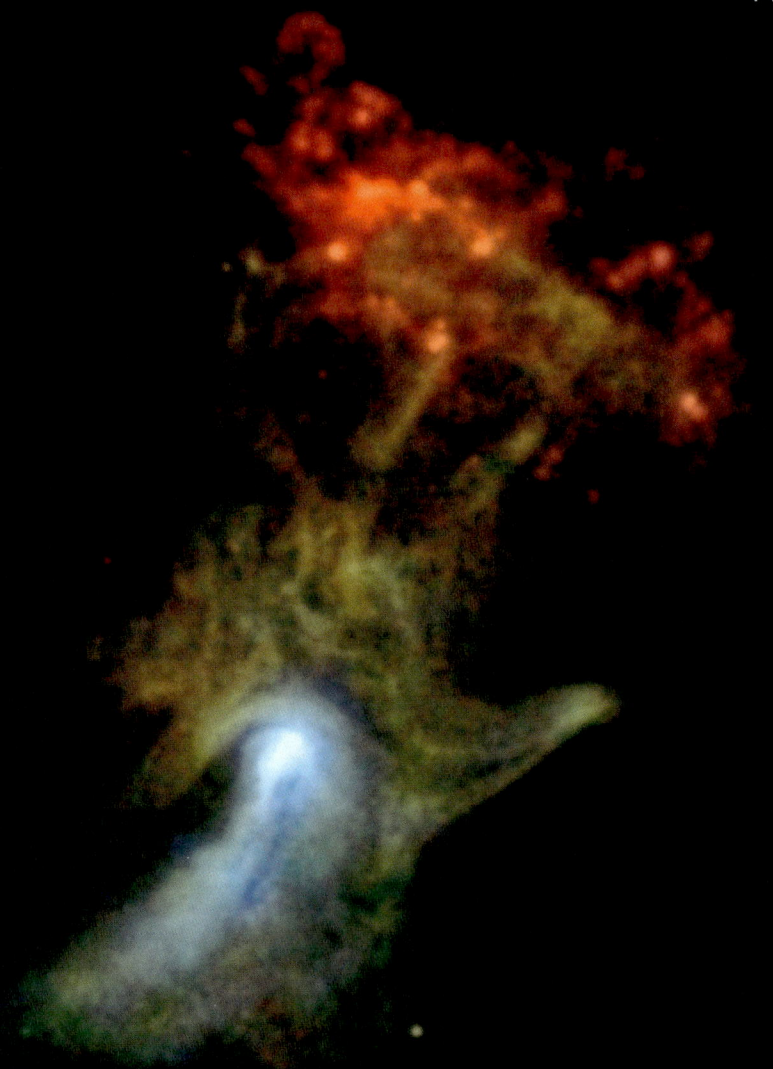

"High-Energy X-ray View of Hand of God"
Photo Courtesy of NASA

PSR B1509-58 nicknamed the "Hand of God", is classified as a pulsar wind nebula. It rotates about 7 times per second, and due to the odd shape of the magnetic field created from the supernova explosion, makes it look like an open hand.

This is the pulsar PSR J1509-5850 and is approximately 12,000 light years away from Earth. It has a long x-ray tail trailing behind it, and a particle trail roughly the same size on the opposite side.

Photo Courtesy of NASA

BLACK HOLES

A black hole is a point in space where gravity pulls so much that even light cannot escape it. Some black holes are created when stars reach the end of their lifespan and collapse in on themselves. The result of this is a supernova; a massive explosion of a dying star that ejects all of its remaining gas into space in spectacular form. What's left of the star's core is very, very small, but it somehow retains all of the gravity of the star before it collapsed, which creates a very small but very dense and powerful region of space that draws everything around it in.

Black Hole Artist Concept
Image Courtesy of NASA

A supermassive black hole is a black hole that can be hundreds of thousands, to *billions* of times the mass of our sun! Black holes can generate jets of all kinds of matter as seen here. The white spot in the middle of the image is a galaxy, where the large orange clouds are x-ray and radio data to visualize the giant plumes of radiation being thrown out by the supermassive black hole in the center of the galaxy.

Photo Courtesy of NASA

This is an x-ray image of the "black hole bounty" near the center of our galaxy. This bounty is theorized to have as many as 20,000 stellar mass black holes, all within 3 light years of the supermassive black hole at the center of the Milky Way!

Photo Courtesy of NASA

This is an artists conception of an event called ASASSN-14li, where there was a star that came too close to a black hole and was torn apart. The formation of the disk was caused by incoming and outgoing streams of star material resulting from the collision.

Image Courtesy of NASA

SUPERNOVAS

A supernova is when a star explodes at the end of its life cycle. It happens when the energy being created in the core (the star's nuclear fusion) cannot hold the core against its own gravity. When this happens, the core collapses and the star explodes into a massive cloud of energy and gas. In the year 1604, Kepler's Star exploded into a supernova that was visible by the naked eye!

This image shows remains of the oldest documented supernova: RCW 86

Photo Courtesy of NASA

Photo Courtesy of NASA

Supernova 1987A has been fascinating to astronomers for quite some time. It was found to have been the brightest star explosion in more than 400 years and burned with the brightness of 100 million suns for several months after the initial explosion, first seen in 1987. It has been amazing astronomers with its light show ever since and has allowed astronomers to study the different phases of a supernova explosion in great detail. On top of all of that, it has been the closest supernova to Earth in hundreds of years.

Photo courtesy of NASA

Seen here is the supernova remnant N 63A. This supernova is part of a star birthing region in a galaxy 160,000 light years away. Usually, supernovas can actually help other stars form when the shockwave hits nearby gases and dust, forcing them together. However, this supernova remnant has proven to be rather destructive and has been destroying nearby gases.

Photo Courtesy of NASA

G292.0+1.8 is one of only 3 supernova remnants in the Milky Way that contains oxygen. These oxygen rich supernovas are especially interesting to astronomers as oxygen is a key part of human life. It is about 20,000 light years away.

And Beyond….

The wonders of the universe in which we live stretch out beyond our imagination. The mysteries of the vast reaches of interstellar space are waiting to be unlocked by future discoveries and the hard work and determination of astronomers both young and old. We hope you have enjoyed this journey Beyond Our Solar System and look forward to future expeditions into the unknown!

If you enjoyed this book please feel free to reach out to us at caelixpublishing@gmail.com. We would LOVE to hear from you!

Happy Travels!

Made in the USA
Monee, IL
19 November 2020